THE MEANING OF COYOTES

THE MEANING
OF COYOTES

POEMS BY WILLIAM MILLS

1984

LOUISIANA STATE UNIVERSITY PRESS

BATON ROUGE AND LONDON

Library of Congress Cataloging in Publication Data
Mills, William, 1935–
   The meaning of coyotes.
   I. Title.
PS3563.I4234M4   1984   811'.54   84-9998
ISBN 0-8071-1193-7
ISBN 0-8071-1196-1 (pbk.)

"The Meaning of Coyotes," "Rituals Along the Arkansas," and "The White Tents of Arctic Summer" appeared previously in *Southern Review*, XX (Fall, 1984).

For Beverly, again

CONTENTS

I

II

1

SOME LINES FOR A HOPI WOMAN

In this cold month's terrain of time
Cancer's footmen seem to be everywhere.
Down the street in both directions my neighbors are dying.
At times the brave or banal ways to death
Converge and swell to nodes of seeing.

I am summoned to a summer past
When I held your woman skull
In the mountains of Arizona.
You, or what there was of you,
And a baby girl
I took to be your own.
I had dug both of you gently
In the hot Arizona day.

In this present research I turn your skull
Hoping the sun's rays will light the rosetta of death.
I think the sacred elements
Have become clearer by this skullduggery.
I see your daily Hopi life,
The carried water, the air clear enough
To see a god in.

Because of you the most unmagic of circles
Which is death seems less strange.
Here, holding your head in my head
The circle widens past my dying friends,
The light of death sweeping beyond you in Arizona,
Past the man with only stone,
Until the speeding circle is everywhere—
Charged by the center of me now.

ON BEING INSTRUCTED BY A NUDE

Your familiar nude had instructed me
Many nights and days before this afternoon.
Your breasts, at times almost translucent
Moving high above me as you made your point,
Or then below me, resting like two sleeping animals.

Your peasant legs that have held me rapt,
And carried you toward me
And sometimes away,
Have carried children, skillets, bushels of grief
And hold the hope that love's sometimes ashes
Can build like limestone a higher place.

With such haunch and leg, such back and breast
It's good that old Rubens can't leave his century.
He'd have you lolling on some superfluous cloud,
Your yellow hair wasted on an angel
While you shiver in the cold Antwerp studio.

You instruct this substantial earth,
And this summer afternoon,
And me as you stand nude in the sun
Casting for our supper's trout,
Your brown body gathering the world to it.
As you gather fish
The world to be fished falls silent.

THE MEANING OF COYOTES

We were trying to get the rocks to speak
In northern Arizona.
Time stretched as far as we could work backward
With the pieces of yesterday
Sifted in our screens,
Left for us to interpret.
The Hopis left us only with hard things,
No song,
But the hafted point,
The killing intention
That ran before it like lightning
Now cooled in flint.

Strange the hunger we have
For the early ones,
Like hounds running their quarry's tracks backwards.

We sat by the fire in the long evening.

Suddenly off the dark mountainside
A coyote's yapping-howl
Stilled everything.
Another howl, answering
From the other side of the valley.
Whether they gathered to love
Or to kill,
They spoke to each other
And they spoke to us,
Taking us past the hafted point,
The song.

RITUALS ALONG THE ARKANSAS

For Robert Lowery

By the first hour we knew the day's luck
Would leave us time to think about each fish.
Not a day when even the unskilled
Pulls fish after fish into a thoughtless boat.

Mindful, we worked the rock jetties
Dragging our baits through the waters
Of a fast Arkansas.
Sometimes it was a rock bass,
Sometimes a white.

But it was the final fish
We held out for—the black,
His barrel of a mouth
Waiting like a mine.
We moved to the pools at the river's edge,
Full of tangle, full of food.
We knew he waited to eat there
Or be eaten.

The priests of do, we sat patiently,
Working our rods with solemnity
And form and always hope,
The idea of Fish large in our minds
Awaiting its marriage to fish.

We brought only water to keep it simple,
The beer was for another time.
Lowery caught the biggest and should have.
His study has been longer.
This black seemed not to want to leave his world below.
But he rose up and danced the bottom of the boat.
That brought the morning to a proper end.

We lay each glistening bass,
Rock, white and black,
On the cleaning board at the boat's side
And prepared their bodies for our use.
First the great heads with their lidless eyes
Were slipped overboard, and then the skin and the bones,
Set to drift through the live waters
Feeding the underworld.

There on the wooden board I poured water
Over the mound of luminous white meat.
As I laid my hands on the meat
To pack it away Lowery looked up river.
"Looks like Canadians flying."
The sight of the big birds
Lining toward us made me forget my duty.
As they drew nearer we knew
We had read the signs wrong.
"Pelicans, white pelicans," he cried.

The line turned into a great spiral of birds
Riding thermals above us:
The utterly no sound, no bird cry,
Only whisper of their outstretched wings
Above our boat, above the Arkansas.
There in the high summer sun
Their great helix of white
Drew fish and man with them.
We are wedded to what we use,
What we love, what we find beautiful.

LINE DRAWING

Living in these fertile hills
I have noticed the repetition
Of certain things.
Some come in sets of four,
Some two, some three:
Finite sets of things
That when repeated
Sometimes seem a circle,
Sometimes a square.

This has given me some peace
And I expect one should take that
Where one finds it,
Spring day, fall day,
Putting the seeds in the ground,
Taking them back.

There are days when I wish
To break from these closed figures
And see a straight line.
West of Stillwater
Is a little what I mean.

Some feel a straight line
Cannot say as much to the mind
As circles or squares—
Like Oklahoma next to Arkansas.
But on some days a straight line
That never stops
Seems to promise.
And promise.

OKLAHOMA YOGA

Stepping across the barbed wire
With rifle and thermos
I will wait for the unpredictable morning
Here in the moonlit pasture.

White-tailed deer will search their way
Through the annual noise
And I will point and be pointed.
This field of pearl light is a way to the target.

Broken by the beginning sun, the field changes.
This cedar windbreak helps these bones
Endure the waiting
While the dark loveliness
Lightens to the inventions
Of red, orange and blood.
Behind this screen
I wait to lunge with my love,
Tightening to the focused shot.

The icy morning drives me inward
Here on the log, here behind the break.
Yet I must search the field,
The intention of my mind
Matching the splendor
Which will come before me:
Swiftly, a brown rush,
Or trembling, nose up, then down, easy.

In the cold sapless grass
He will come striding, radiant,
Running against the slope of the world's drift,
The aura firing out like divinity.

I think of companions hidden among the hills
Waiting with me, of the bedroll I left.
I jerk myself back to focus.
Breathe deeply and hold it
And let it out slowly.
Thoughts of my old sergeant
Intone the sutra of shooting:
Breathe in again, wipe the mirror clean,
Lie open to inventions of the field.

I need some Cherokee master to whack me back
To concentration. The world's noise
Keeps coming. Breathe in; hold it; out slowly.

In the rusty light, *now, now,*
The musky one is. Then is running.
We run over the stony Oklahoma slopes
As the fire enters us
And sets us free.

Hunting the stony, snowy slopes of Oklahoma
Tests the reasons for our being here.
It is January and not moderate November
With its burnishes of brown and red.
Sitting before the fire last night
Hunting seemed the only choice.
Now there is no fire to be seen.

With the high grass mostly gone
The dogs range wide,
Their moving on the prairie
Sure with instinct and hope.
The cold concentrates both
Dog hunter, man hunter,
And the snow shows the skeleton
Of bushes more clearly.
This white seems the absence
Against which all things
Come as they are.

Even we can see the quails' tracks in the snow,
Like a virgin breaking,
Like first word, first sign
Toward that which is there.

But the tracks disappear and we know
Who must lead us through this
Invisible labyrinth of scent,
Crafted by the covey we must find.
The oldest dog is the shaman
And we follow full of faith.

He leads down a draw
And our following drops slowly

Through the cleft earth deeply,
The sides rising above till we
Lose sight of the land.
The underearth opens with scent
As the shaman of dogs works in a frenzy
This calculus of passage,
Dog and man tracking what is
On and under the world.
It is a test of sense
And failure will be kept
Where it hurts the most.

Now our shaman disappears over the rim
His retinue scrambling clumsily after.

There on the snowy plain
Our pointer, stiffened to the world,
Sculpted by desire,
Becomes the geometry of desperate economy.

There with the world's energy arcing
Between pointer and pointed,
I watch the birds break to beauty.
The design of survival is desire.

SCULPTURE OF WATER

The summer was besotted with the wrong neighbors.
I wanted to take vengeance on them for being mine;
They took vengeance on me for being theirs.

The earth and sky, the water and air
Were drunk with city foulings.

This battle line for beauty stalemated, you and I
Shifted our tactics and headed
For the Feliciana hills to the north.
You would fish, your passion; I would reconnoiter
The pines and creeks.

Baited and busy on the raft, your concentration
For bass and bream was serious.
I left you shed of your clothes under an abundant sun.

In the shallowest of creeks
I lay on my back and became the water.
Under the leaf-green the minnows
Nibbled my body.

The smallest of winds
And the kindest of clear water
Quieted the mind's racket.

Later I came to you on the raft.
You there, almost fishless,
The only nude fisher in the county,
And the tenor and bass frogs,
A pileated woodpecker and the shy crows.

We began to rock on the raft,
Slowly carving a sculpture of water
While we moved steadily at the center.

Louisiana air. Between water and fog.
It drowns me in the windlessness of my age.
In October there should be a bite,
A definition of what lies before me:
Brown pecan leaves, cut hay fields.

The thick weather instead reminds me
I have not gone where I intended to go.

I have arrived
Where I thought those who had looked
And thought hard before me
Knew what they were doing.

Here I am in their place.
I don't even recognize the road.

THREE SPARROWS CIRCLED IN A DUSTY DANCE

The Louisiana afternoon was swollen with heat
Holding off a thousand creature sounds
Waiting for the release of dusk.

Still there was the expected jay,
The distant telegraphic crow, ubiquitous sparrows,
A summer's quotient.

Suddenly the sparrows' voices changed
Saying in this minor key
Something not ever heard by me.

I assumed an itinerant cat, felt a nagging fear
And went out to see. There was no cat,
Yet whatever charged these sparrows was charging me.

And there upon the path
Three sparrows circled in a dusty dance
The center held by a black, magnetic snake.

The three sparrows had given up the air
And returned to hop hypnotically upon the ground,
Weaving closer, closer, then away.

The drowsing snake seemed content, unawares,
Like a languorous woman sunbathing in a private place,
Taking any worship as her due.

The bands that held the sparrows to the snake
Seemed taut with magic, seemed to hold the world,
As if the world's entropic downward drift

Were turned around with this new energy
Like some terrible love that holds the world of live,
As I am held by the sparrow and the snake.

PLAQUEMINE POINT

From this vantage point
Blocked from the river by the levee,
I can only hear the towboat
Making its way slowly upstream.
I imagine the twinscrews
Roiling the caramel water,
The lighted cabins passing squares of light.

On this side of the levee the Brahmans
Graze in the final summer light
And some calf thinks it's lost its mother.
A twelve-month heifer nurses an errant cow.
The ring-eyed bull busies himself with flies.

Living on Plaquemine Point has focused this existence.
Living on a point often does.
To save time, not many travel
This longer, looping way.

There is no denying for me the palpability
Of the levee grass, the voices of the cows,
The thick Louisiana clouds between me
And the loosening sun.
That there may be anything behind this
Is the point.

A gray horse in the foreground,
A green levee with red Brahmans the background.

Also important:
The ground that comes before both
With me in it,
Intending to know more
About red Brahmans and a gray horse
By looking carefully at both.
Like the first time.

Red casual dots,
A gray horizontal
Crossing Cartesian gradients,
Becoming rounds and flourishes.

Then gratitude,
To be looked at more closely.

ANNIVERSAIRE TROPIQUE

The Royal Street gardens strain with green.
June brides here have a thick
Burden girls from Oregon never know.
Heaviness of the tropics.

Birthdays in this heat toll like funerals,
Counting what's left, not where I've been.
The idea of winter vamps the citizens
With the promise of sweet painful winds.

Wisteria invades me like river fog
Through old French houses. Forever
The without, the within are too close.
How can my chilly heart change this weather?

GOING FOR THE LIGHT

Always the light at some sudden hour
Could take our breath away
—Stalled briefly
Holding the scene up to Florence or Rome.
In the French Quarter
On the balcony on Royal Street
Where we watched
The nighthawk's evening swings,
Our hearts swelled
Like mushrooms after rain,
And we seemed to rise upward
Toward the center
Of all things.

We sat before an October fire
In the hardwoods.
The wind blessed us by not blowing.
A half-moon pearled the fields;
Our tent stood in the woods.
Something fell and should have:
An acorn, a limb, a star.
We understood the fire as it settled.

SILHOUETTE

When I was six and plundering primary school
The week long, my parents kept me to yard
Till supper and bed. Saturday, though, it was over
To John B's for ball and bat or soldiers

The Germans the bad ones again. Released from school,
Loose from my own yard, from my mother's eyes,
Away from the teacher's eyes where I tried to keep
The capitals big and the long words on the pages.

One rainy Saturday, the mother of John B,
If not to be saved by bayonet or ball
Was not to be subdued. She took out
Scissors and paste and thick construction paper.

Was this to be school again? No. One, then the other,
Laid his head down while she traced around them,
Then cut out who we were, the scissors snipping
Around the top and the eyes, over the nose,

The lips and chin, down to the Adam's apple.
(So much attention paid, so much demanded).
How I marveled at the artist of that afternoon,
And marveled at me, the way I had never seen me.

She pasted this white image on a sheet
Of black paper and stuck it on the wall.
No one could read my eyes, a statue's eyes,
And I have not since seen so clearly what I am.

BLACK AND BLUE
For Mike Hills

Fifty now
And Korea behind us
Like a bill too old to collect
We stand on this beach
Of the Gulf of Mexico
In crisp February,
Air like the clarity
We had always hoped for.

Then the clear world
Slowly turned,
Became blue, became gray.
Still beautiful.

Simply surviving
For this slate gray happiness
Was what we wanted.
Of course we did not say this.

BOARDS

I have been watching my neighbor's house
Receive and give back a little
Oklahoma sunset in very late October.

This landscape celebrates browns
From a risky palette
New England never tries.

What happens on the shiplapped
Boards facing west
Floods my heart with
Sun color and wood.

I welcome soon the sinking light
As it eases this ecstasy,
As the natural selection of sun and wood
Leads itself to conclusion,
Giving me time to ponder
This fusion.

SOON YOU WILL AWAKE

At four in the morning
I reach for your foot, your thigh,
Anything to tell me
I am here at four in the morning.

I think the common thoughts
Of me without you in dark after dark.

I taste my saliva and swallow,
Thinking of that gray chill
That unblesses two corpses
Who once loved each other.

Having held you
I must get hold of myself.
Soon you will awake.
I must celebrate this
With a pageant of coffee and oranges.

ON HEARING OF THREE CHIMPS
DEAD BY FIRE IN A RESEARCH TRAILER
WHILE UNDERGOING LANGUAGE TRAINING

No doubt the cages were quiet
Because of the hour,
A little humming in the adjacent lab.
Entering the room,
You might have expected to see the young female
Using her hands to mean "banana,"
Asking your name.

When smoke filled the room,
When fire (as if from the African forest)
Filled the room,
What sculpture did her hands make?

Half deaf and slower
I never know when someone is calling.

Is it a phone or desire
I say hello to?
This black instrument of my dream
That reaches no one.

Does the mind blow now?

The year had begun like a wishbone,
Promise running ahead on its tracks.
It had been a spring whistled by every jay
For miles, but it was the mockingbird
You heard.
Your brood fell out of the house
And into the streets with their hoodly boys
While you stood like Mrs. Lot,
Salty and frozen in high summer,
Always looking back to a swollen past
Fetid with dead dreams.

After the fall, the winter, of course.
You sit before the fire, grateful to have a fire,
Not holding the bag but the small end of wishing,
Like one knitting needle
And half a sweater.

QUIETING THE OLD FEAR
OF LIVING IN A FILM

After watching the film about the lions
Dragging the torn carcass of the kudu at the waterhole,
Some observations:
I was grateful to the cameraman
For his being there.
But without the smell of the lion
And the kudu
This scene urged itself toward abstraction,
For death has a smell as life slides from hot to cold.

It may be some new technique
Will include the scent
And even the touch of the lion's lips
On the kudu's breast.

Then it may be difficult
To know the difference,
What is, and is repeated.

DISTANT FIRE

In the beginning
You were far away.
You could be steered by
Like a distant sun,
Could be hope, desire,
The lead in a godly story.

Close to you now
I feel like the moth
Who knew his way for millions of years
By his angle to the sun or moon.
Until we brought the light too close.
The moth appears foolish now.

II

UNLOADING IN VIENNA

We met in a Hapsburg's bedroom
While filing through the halls of what he called home in
   Vienna,
You from Australian outback,
Me from sultry Louisiana.

Out of the unfamiliar opulences
We made our way through the damp-cold
Loaded Austrian air,
Both of us strangers to this weather.

We felt protected by the secret society of transients,
We who always brought out with us what we brought in.
My train would be the first to leave
And we talked out the hours
On a bench among ducks.

There beneath the clouds releasing their snow
The epiphany of transients
Made the unmarked bench a holy place.

Time began its contractions
And there before winter ducks
We told each other stories
We would not tell familiars,
Those who have been suffered,
And suffered with us
The warfare and welfare of the daily rounds.

LEAVING SZENTENDRE

On the train back to Budapest
I think of the old Serbian Merchant's house,
A gallery now for the new artists.
That and the bare remains of the Roman encampment
Overshadowed by the secondary school.

Outside the train window,
Far from anything, a boy
Plays with his dog in the middle
Of the white field.
No house, no road.
Only the boy and his dog leaving tracks.

I ask you what is the name
Of those mountains.

"Viserad."

"Viserad," I say.
Then, "Danube, Szentendre."
In the face of that snowy field
I see myself the boy without the dog.

THE POPLARS PERPENDICULAR

The poplars perpendicular
Blinked one and one and one
Past our speeding car
As we abandoned Lake Balaton that fall.
You were far away even then, even in that car
Hurtling sadly toward Budapest.

Except for the flame of one urgent
Pheasant cock who hurried overhead,
All was cold.

The staccato of trees still speaks to me.
I have worried these monoliths
From dream to dream.

They slowed as they fell behind
In the car's mirror,
Became a steady state,
Like those far ahead
That seemed no part
Of these blurred trees
Whipping past.

I think I understand these upright trees.
They say come here, come here,
They say go away.

MOSCOW

The snow in the rail yard
Was a blanket
Cut by the lines
Our train would follow
To Orsha and Vilnius.

In my compartment
I wondered what to do with Red Square
And Lenin's tomb,
The chapels of the bell towers.
Time settled on me
Like a winter's fog.

I lowered the window
Driven to the fresh snowy air.

You in the other train,
You in your plain uniform
Shy at first,
Surer as my leaving
Was certain,
Flirted and called out
In the peasant cold.

Afraid of police
And every other rumor I believed,
I stared
Until your bravery broke through.

I flashed the highball sign—OK—
And you disappeared,
Perhaps wondering
About my three straight fingers,
And the circle beside them.

I am only one airport away
Moving west in the thin air
Knowing something of you is moving with me.

Your smell and juices
From the last morning bed
I still carry. The taste
Of your lipstick I carry, too.

I see your form blossoming in a hundred petals:
In the sleeping car from Rovaniemi,
Blush and shiny in our wooden sauna,
Watching me eat reindeer fawn at the tavern.

On cross-country skis
You kept calling hurry up.

Now one of us is left behind.
You in Helsinki, you behind all
I carry in the plane—
Or me behind this idea of you.

(How lonely the mind that may
Hold the world.)

The idea of you has never been
To fifty-five degrees, twelve minutes before,
Then fifty-four degrees, six minutes,
Arcing to the west
At thirty-five thousand feet,
Faster than the earth's turning.

(What a paucity transcendence is.)

No idea will ever do:
Only palpable you.

NEW YEAR'S IN BUDAPEST

I

In the Metro the children blew their paper horns,
An Italian kissed the lady engineer.
The brown Danube was loosening its loins.

Above ground we rode our tram by rote.

Down the clotted sidewalk ran a soldier,
His green-braided hat askew, blood streaming from his ear,
His tunic the season's color.

Behind him came two waiters in their white coats.

The reason for all this running? As long time prints
The plot, no consequence, no doubt. His story unreels
By the frames of our car to the vanishing point.

II

Yet their lives mostly mime
The tram car of their time,
The stars invisible half, half only dots.
Our average terror comes not
From looking into space
But each into the other's face.

We hold on tight
As the tram car bumps the night,
Remembering the bloody soldier running away,
Knowing the white coats will always make him pay.

SLOW MAYAN THUNDER

For Martin and Delores Prechtel

Slow Mayan thunder
And rain on a tin roof.
An Indian's skirt on the line
That flapped its reds and yellows
Now relaxes like me
In the Antiguan twilight.

The schoolchildren drummed and thumped
Around the town today
Practicing for a saint's day.
Dat-dat, dat-dat tum. Te deum.
What might be a dirge
Is undone by the cymbal bells
And the calves of the majorettes.
They fade to the edge of town.

I have not learned to welcome
The final day's colors and drums
With such slow peace,
But the breeze off the cool mountains
Dries my day's sweat
As I stare at a faraway Ceiba tree.

ARCTIC CIRCLE

Beyond the doubled windows
The cars are humped white
In the powdered snow
Like you, moonlit in this bed.

White here rushes toward me, then
Away like certain memories of you.

The silence stretches in Lapland
Until one's step crunches the snow,
Then gone, then again.

Outside, the sturdy firs
Carry their burden of bright ice
In the long Finnish night.

Old lovers us, children gone,
We have stood our fierce ground,
Arms outstretched for the sun.

ARCTIC PHOTOGRAPHER

Golden Plover

As I go toward you
You go away—
Away with a broken wing act
You desperately believe in,
Must, with four eggs warming you,
Eggs you warm.

I'd been prepared for the play,
An old ritual.

You lead over the broken rocks
Into tamarack and willow.
"Over here! Here is what you want,
Me, wounded and available. Over here!"

Finally I sit long enough
For you to become accustomed to one
Who comes only to watch,
Only to take your image.

Semipalmated Plover

From where you sit in the small rocks
Over the green-brown eggs
What springs from the shape
Coming upon you?
Half-palmated, half-afraid and sure,
What will this do to you
Who only flew from South America
To this arctic esker,
Having given most of everything
For a reason you cannot call a reason?

What is this,
The shape that kneels
And looks into your eye
Shining in the tundra sun?

ROCK, SNOW, BEAR, SKY

The bears are mounds of white
In the arctic night,
The foxes move silently,
Their tails settled with soft snow.
The moon is a promise,
The wind sure.

Here
Surrounded by the tundra night
And the best of men
I have by this cold simplicity
Prepared myself for everywhere.

The roar and white water at the Portage
Concatenate here by this boulder,
Surging from a source I have never seen.
Only old trappers and Indians have been there.

The boulder is limed with gull droppings,
Signs of their watching, their fishing
For what they need.
I am watchful too of what I need
Here at the Portage
In the steady thunder and thrashing.

In the river onward,
In the never-stop of power
Can beauty stop?

And what does the osprey feel
As he dives,
Claws in the icy waters?

At sunset now the spruce
Finger the sky.
On high ground a friend grills our trout
In the curling smoke.
The gulls drift
In the thermals of evening.

I have walked this northern island we camp on,
Felt full of the blue vetch meadows,
    the granite rocks.
In my walking I startled sandpipers and geese
On their nests.
Did beauty first come
Like an intruding stranger in a blue meadow?

I wonder if beauty has ever come to the osprey
Diving into the water?

The arctic terns wheel by
Turning me again toward gratitude
For all that fly, swim, move and eat
On the river.

THIS WHITE OUTLINE OF
OUR HUNTING: HUDSON BAY

For Fred Bruemmer

The morning started with a river
Only lately able to move.
From the stillness in white
The bay cracked awfully
Releasing a river of the Barrens.

Red char swam the white banks
Like young virgin blood—
Bright and doomed.

We prowled the floes
Looking for the black dots
Of dozing seals.
These Innuits were beyond the time
Of harpoons purely.
Harpoons come now
After the rifle shot,
After the race to resurrect the black body
Out of the emerald arctic waters
For the ritual slaughter.

After the body came to the boat
We gathered for tea and bannock on the ice.
The Coleman stove bubbled water
As the harpoonist turned his knife
To the gentle surgery.

As the skin curled outward
The flesh looked like a custard
Children would want.

Children who were there on the ice
Watched it like the first time
For all men.

All day there had been no sound
But ice thunder, rifle shot.
We stood circling the fire
On the ice with smoking tea in our hands
Thinking some great thing would fill
This white outline of our hunting.

Coming upon them for the first time
I knew they meant more than shelter.
Each tent was a block of white
Stuck on the horizon,
The flat eternity of the tundra,
An abstract swelled with meaning.

Wandering in the Mondrian landscape
Near one of those solitary tents
I came suddenly upon a wooden rack
Lined with the red bright bodies of drying fish
And the drying brown hips and hooves
Of a caribou.
It seemed as if Bruegel might have sauntered by
And twisted the scene to his liking,
But out of the tent
Came a family of four
Parka-ed and booted against the razor wind.

Over tea and bannock freely given
I asked about the tents
(Though not just like that)
And the father said it was noisy
In the village, the air was bad.

Hard times I knew had drawn his people down
To those government houses rowed neatly by the bay.
But they were Padlermiuts—
Caribou Eskimos of the Barrens.
Their land had always stretched forever,
Forever in a special silence.

He smiled,
Admitting he had been once in the forest

Many years ago, but did not like it much.
"You couldn't see far in such a place."

Likewise he couldn't see far in such a town.

Come June, the air blew in from the Barrens
Cooking with smells,
And the village emptied,
One by quiet one,
Going where the old ghosts could visit,
Where under the white tents
That held onto the tundra
There was tea and bannock.

LORDS

For the members of the Cape Churchill expeditions

I

Nose high over the ice rim
He was. No sound in the arctic morning,
Moving as if the whole white world
Were his, a majesty of generations.
The slight northern sun
Let the bear's aura flame out
As he trudged the jagged ice
Toward us on our guarded perch;
We had come to behold the white lord.

Like any god he would devour us
Were we not beyond his reach.
Yet we leaned toward him,
As close as his breath.
(How tantalizing, the black lips!)
Staring now at the great head,
Now into the hot opaque brown eyes
We plumb the heart of wildness
In a cold white land.

Some among us come not only for awe;
Some come to measure,
To send reports to that place
Where all numbers are gathered.

Not satisfied with the simple telemetry of grandeur,
They want to know wherefore the lord,
How and how much.

II

Abrupting across the silent land
The helicopter whirls low

Bearing these curious men
Who mean to leave no mystery unturned.

Swooping, the swirling bird
Unleashes its dose of angel dust,
Hovers—while the lord stumbles and falls—
Then lights near the body.
The inquisitive come out,
Guns drawn in the pale light.

III

Prostrate before you,
Every orifice violated,
You learn my heat,
My breath strokes, my age.
I cannot close my eyes
Before what you do.

As long as you have known yourself as man
You have tried to put on my power,
My head on your own head
In skull-lined caves across the world.

You try to take it on now
By numbering each piece of this world,
And in a distant moment
To hold all pieces in mind,
To be done
With the stink and stature of bear.

IV

You step back
As I begin to move.

You gather in groups for life's only reason,
To bring the big animal down.

But I must be kept alive,
Who know cold as you have never known it,
Who even taught The People how to hunt.
Without me you walk in deserts.
Imprison me, you cage yourselves.

Again now up from within myself,
Up from the gulag of limits
To the pure white dream.

Bounding the eskers fingering the sea
I go to meet the seal to be killed,
Who awaits me like a lover.

Rising up from this sleep
I assume myself.

I move out among the toothed sea rocks
Of the receded tide,
The frozen rocks like flowers.
Whale killer, strider of ice,
The Alpha of my retinue
Of foxes, ravens and gulls, and
Now you who need me too.
We die, we devour each other,
We live to die again.